# Speaking Without Tongues

JANE MONSON

Published by Cinnamon Press
Meirion House
Glan yr afon
Tanygrisiau
Blaenau Ffestiniog
Gwynedd, LL41 3SU
www.cinnamonpress.com

The right of Jane Monson to be identified as author of this work has been asserted by her in accordance with the Copyright, Designs and Patent Act, 1988. Copyright © 2010 Jane Monson
ISBN: 978-1-907090-22-6

British Library Cataloguing in Publication Data. A CIP record for this book can be obtained from the British Library.
*All rights reserved. No part of this publication may be reproduced, stored in a retrieval system, or transmitted in any form or by any means, electronic, mechanical, photocopying, recording or otherwise without the prior written permission of the publishers. This book may not be lent, hired out, resold or otherwise disposed of by way of trade in any form of binding or cover other than that in which it is published, without the prior consent of the publishers.*

Designed and typeset in Palatino by Cinnamon Press. Cover from original artwork 'Clock Tower Silhouette' by Stasyuk Stanislav, designed by Cottia Fortune-Wood.

Printed in Poland

Cinnamon Press is represented in the UK by Inpress Ltd www.inpressbooks.co.uk and in Wales by the Welsh Books Council www.cllc.org.uk.

The publisher acknowledges the financial assistance of the Welsh Books Council

# Acknowledgements

For their time, support and focus, my appreciation and thanks to: Martin Coyle, Stephen Logan, Andy Brown, Luke Kennard, Richard Gwyn, John Freeman, Carrie Etter, Phil Robins, Kate North and Josie Pearse. Essential support and insight also came from my writing groups in London and Cambridge, the Muswell Hill Bookshop, Jon O'Connor, Lindsay Fursland, Clare Sims, CB1, Maria Scott and family, and Daniel Monson.

Finally my excitement and appreciation goes to Jan Fortune-Wood and Cinnamon Press for their engaged part in the development of the contemporary prose poem in English.

# Contents

| | |
|---|---|
| Church Falls | 9 |
| Defying Gravity | 10 |
| Via Negativa | 11 |
| Hatching | 12 |
| Grandmother's Footsteps | 13 |
| The Sandman | 14 |
| Babysitting | 16 |
| Cloud Food | 18 |
| The Nightmare | 19 |
| The Astrayed | 20 |
| The Unheard | 21 |
| The Unmended | 22 |
| Sarah's Sandals | 23 |
| What Death Said | 24 |
| Ghost in the Stone | 25 |
| My Father's Garden | 26 |
| Family Portrait | 27 |
| The Mending Wall | 28 |
| Christ: Crouch End | 30 |
| The Prose Poem | 31 |
| The Swallow Myth | 32 |
| Falling Out of the Wood | 33 |
| Weather Quartet | 34 |
| Station Butterflies | 35 |
| Indoor Skies | 36 |
| Bridgesong | 37 |
| The Seasoned Listener | 38 |
| Hunger | 39 |
| The Herd | 40 |
| The Handwritten | 41 |
| Little Sisyphus | 42 |
| The Cry in the Wall | 43 |
| Blood Cycle | 44 |

| | |
|---|---|
| The Pale Glass Wall | 45 |
| Alice Aphasia | 45 |
| The Lesson | 47 |
| The Estranged | 48 |
| Blackwater | 49 |
| Speaking without Tongues | 50 |
| The Speaking Cloth | 51 |
| The Clock | 52 |
| Peter's Pica | 53 |
| Unannounced Visitors | 54 |
| Kierkegaard's Chairs | 55 |
| The Silent Trade | 56 |
| Object Poem | 57 |
| 'I, Poppy' | 58 |
| Gutter-cup | 59 |
| Fossilized | 60 |
| Visible Speech | 61 |

*In memory of my parents,
Sarah and Paul*

# Speaking Without Tongues

# Church Falls

The roof quotes Gothic, then Romanesque. The floor understands neither, its aisled stone tongue cracked and splintered, each flag its own fit. The ground looks starved. Rugs are cast like bones; the dips and folds make flesh or skeleton of the faces that pattern the cloth. Each look is of a tight or a loose order according to the flow of the weave. Smoke contorts above the fabric, then cuts out and sinks into the design. Incense fills the unstitched gaps. Stutters from the organ mark the air. The minister opens his mouth as if to yawn, falls away from the lectern; static returns in his voice.

A marble falls from the pocket of a boy and tells us where the rug ends and the stone begins; he lifts another to his smile and swallows it, tugs at his mother's sleeve. Tugs again.

# Defying Gravity

They are being called inside, politely yet patiently, by a young, tired looking woman who stands on the doorstep, one hand on the door-frame, the other rising towards her hair. The girl crouches, her green jumper arched smooth over her back, her palms moving, shifting flowers over the pavement, and the boy stands with his arms above his head, grinning, his tee-shirt riding over his belly, petals stopped across his hair. The sky has come into bloom and they are catching the pieces that fall. The woman shouts, steps forward – the blossom rises, spins around the children as they move in awkward twists, like pine trees thrashing in snow. Shadows stretch like elastic from their feet – they are keeping the whiteness in the air, shouting at it to fly until they are covered, until they are satisfied by its magic, until it has browned; has bruised from their kicks and hands; torn from their open mouths. The woman shouts again, is crossing the road, squinting, resisting laughter; pulling the shadows behind, like dogs at her heels, raising her arms and spreading out her hands, trying to keep the lightness in the air.

# Via Negativa

My mother was not Christ, but she was spat at. My father was not Christ, but he didn't always know this. The two of them met in a garden, but they were not Adam and Eve. And when my mother became pregnant, this was considered a miracle, and when pregnant again, this was nothing short of Blake's sunflower vision. But we are none of these things. When my mother had an epileptic attack, she looked like a monster. Of course, she was not possessed, but as children we didn't always know this. What she was, was spat at. Someone we didn't know, who was more needle than skin, more threadbare than whole, turned his mouth to her as she fitted on the pavement; emptied his tongue, and told her to get up. Beside her, flowers shook their heads behind a newly built wall. She'd made the bricks bleed on her way down, and narrowly missed the plaque that named them the city's best roses.

# Hatching

They would land in the middle of the plate — sometimes on top of the peas — spiders which had lost their grip on the lightshade and fallen. She grew up comparing the glue of a web to a cheap envelope. Her mother, at such dinners, would go red in the face and curse their life; the sound was of flies repeating themselves on a window-pane. The daughter would sit quietly, and ask for each fly to be caught. *Be careful what you bloody well ask for*, her mother once said, and shot the girl a look that landed in her stomach. She had no recollection of speaking aloud, but from that moment started to bite her lip whenever she had these thoughts. Teeth-marks began to form on her mouth, and more flies on the tongue of the mother.

# Grandmother's Footsteps

The racket that jolted us from sleep was of the bathroom breaking into pieces, drums ransacking the sky, conkers bombing the earth, desk-lid protests in class. Next door, we'd sit upright in our beds, stiff as dolls, paralysed by the din of bottles, mugs, toothbrushes, stacks of soap, hairbrushes, lotions, vitamins – everything we'd touched the night before, and been told to put back in place – knocked senseless by your juddering fists and feet.

We were meant to race towards you, stay until the storm had left, and sometimes we did, on the outside. Inside, we'd stop and creep a few pale steps, in the way of the game we'd played at school, whispering on tiptoes up to the Wolf's back.

# The Sandman

Jim was his name, a bright chase of red hair fidgeting around his eyes and over his shoulders. Most of his features were awkward as though he'd fallen and let too many people put him together again, but his eyes were proud, clear and changing, the colours catching you out according to where he was; one minute the skin of lime, the next the fruit. When the mother had left, he listened carefully to the children as they repeated her words. There was no television in the house, but there were games in the cupboard and books in every room. Jim adapted quickly to playing; made sure to include both the boy and the girl equally, laughing and clapping as the boy leapt over chairs, arms outstretched, in flight across the living room floor in his pyjamas, and teasing the girl as she begged her brother to calm down and be quiet. When he began to settle, she unfolded her knees and arms from her chest, got up from her chair, and said she had a game, a trick she wanted to show. The girl had mastered this act alone, but in front of them she kept making mistakes and falling down, so Jim made her practise – head on a cushion on the floor by the wall, palms flat on the carpet either side of her reddening cheeks, she would kick her legs in the air and he would seize her ankles. The backs of her calves against the wall, her feet nearly touching the shelves above, he would let go, clap and watch. When she had perfected the wall, he set the cushion in the centre of the room, and placed her there like a vase. Moving his hands gently from her legs, fingers outstretched, he tiptoed backwards through the air, a green eye on the delicate line cast from her toes to the ceiling, the skin glowing from the hanging light, the nightdress gathered about her neck and face, in still white folds over her eyes and baited breath.

# Babysitting

Anna holds her arms up high while I undress her. In the bathroom she crashes the toothbrush around her teeth, foams at the mouth while I stand in the doorway looking past her head to the form that towers in the mirror. At her bedside, she introduces me to her doll, stabbing a finger at its old cloth body as it lies face down, slung between a pillow and a sleeping cat. I tuck her between the sheets, the black hump of the cat uncurls, moves down the bed and wilts over her legs; she won't be able to feel them later she warns me, and she needs them during her sleep, to outrun the dog who turns the corners of walls, where she is always waiting. I perch on the bed with a book. There are no dogs in here I tell her, only a ship that sails white against the horizon, and carries people over the blue waves into the path of the sun, which melts orange into the sea, and makes the salt turn sweet. Anna brings her knees up to her chest and pulls an old piece of rag through her fingers; her eyes close, but her hand stays awake, coiled around the rag that rests near her neck. I read on through the changes in her breathing, stop when her voice starts to separate from sleep; she is counting aloud, her voice ticking through sequence: one to ten, one to twenty, one to thirty, the numbers building and rebuilding in the dark. When she falls quiet, I hear the rain stuttering at the window, the

growth of a laugh around a corner, and someone outside
coughing, blowing shapes across the walls.


There are no dogs out there, a voice says,
only a white ship heading for the sun
and shrinking
down inside the water like sugar.

# Cloud Food

Childhood was scruffy. A wintered-out coat with the promise of a hood, money inching up the walls of a china pot, views of untidy sea-shores. In the house, we grew amid yellowing spines, and dog-eared covers; a curious collision of titles and names – the outlandish and the refined as worn out as each other – torn and thumbed under the blessing, or curse, of your ravenous eye. This unconditional and indiscriminate love for life in print became the strange ways of our meals. Nights of tatty lettuce, wrung dry over the sink in your hands; jagged vegetables in curries, landing bruised on the plates, airborne and cold. Next door, you'd lie on your stomach by the fire, book in one hand, fork in the other. This silence, your absence, triggered the devil in us. At each supper we'd invite him over the threshold. He taught us to wreck the turning pages, to loathe the sound of you reading; inviting words we didn't understand into your head, walking into other people's homes, laughing at things we never saw, being privy to conversations we couldn't hear. Worst of all, he showed you travelling alone, long before the coppers had lifted the lid off the china pot, and told us that we could all go.

# The Nightmare

A man lets himself into our house – a slick turn of the lock, a weightless foot on the landing. Creeping upstairs to the bathroom, he closes the door and stands in the centre of the room, straight, composed, without light and breath. From the bed I hear him, shifting, then stopping outside my sleep. Leaving the lamp off, I turn back the sheets and try the doors of the rooms, leaning on each handle like an unsure guest. On the steps to the bathroom, I hear him start to breathe behind the wood. Opening the door, pulling hard on the cord, I bring us to life under the glass-shade. Arms by his side, he ignores my horror and speaks. When I open my mouth, the place starts to shout. Boards, walls and ceiling move out from themselves towards me and the man reappears in the corner of the bedroom. He says nothing, but bows his head towards his chest, slow, like a priest. Behind him are my mother's bookshelves. He raises his arms to protect my head, and she appears in the doorway, looking past me through the dust and collapse. My eyes fix on the man in the corner; his loss of breath and dignity beneath all of her books.

# The Astrayed

*My husband died a year ago*
*and there are these gaps in our conversations.*

The woman was looking for a book, but could not remember the name, as it was spoken, as it was given to her over a year ago. She could hear his voice but the words were vague. Like driving on a mountain road in deep mist, she said, hoping the stone didn't stray from beneath you; guessing at the corners, the occasional glimpse of headlights, from dip to dip. Worst of all are the unexpected shapes, the sheep that spring from the sides of a road secluded in fog, where the heart has stopped and strange lights draw in, near and far, like thunder. Turning from the counter she looks behind her and traces the shelves of books in silence. Her neck strains from left to right, a slow side to side deliberation, until something passes through her, bends her head to the floor, and drops her hand to her side. The leather bag on her shoulder slips the length of an arm, and empties around her feet. The world whispers her new ways of telling on the past. She hears out the settling of a coin. Her face is lined, wet, and gleaming. The skin begins to flicker to the beat of a faulty light.

# The Unheard

'How big is our house compared to Russia?' She pivots by the bookshelves, answers with a sort of embarrassed wind in her voice. There are more questions like this that he wants to ask, but he is forced to change tack; tears his fingers across the book spines, sounds them out like piano keys, starting with a shriek and growling low into the earth by the final note. Before he opened his mouth and let Russia out, there was something else he wanted to ask her, or less a question than a wish to convey an excitement, a warmth towards her, their life and their place in the world. She never heard him in public – was always listening to them – but every so often he tested her, tugged her sleeve and said what he heard inside. And then, later at home, before sleep, he'd continue to score the wall in his bedroom with tally charts to keep track of the unheard questions: above the skirting boards, the boy's world was hemmed with nearly two hundred miniature fences. One day, he would pull back the bed, the chest of drawers and his desk and take her through these fences, these gates, these scars and stitches across the paint and see how she would react without listeners; with no one but him and scratches as the eyes and ears of their talk.

# The Unmended

The road is covered in ghost. It is a substance unlike web or dust, but closer to an externalised thought – an old thought pulled out from sleep, shaken and spread across the stone. The land begins to shift in tremors. Underneath the beat of metal and wind, blasts of memory rise and fall. A hood of a coat. The cracked face of a watch. The ticking wheel of a bicycle. The stream of traffic, frozen. The air drained of noise, filled back up to the brim with wailing. Blood has stopped inside her hood to dry, dreaming red and slow from her hair. The outline of her body shivers in and out of view. She tries to hibernate from memory; random things emerge her. She is tired of ghosting this road. With no lines to learn. Just a rude awakening from the eves, to play out the same cue, the final act before the curtain. The same person in the audience, unable to clap, unable to leave, shouting, *encore, encore.*

# Sarah's Sandals

The leather straps that fed through your metal buckles were tired and coiled from season after season of reliance: when one day saw you in another pair it was as though you'd thrown your feet away.

Across your high-boned ridge, the tan-straps rose, peaked and dug into your skin; ephemeral red scars the patterns and traces of your spirit, while underneath, the unexposed landscapes of your heels gravitated black and pitted into the soles.

When your sandaled feet left the ground for good they were balanced mid-air, mid-winter on the pedals of a blue-steel bicycle, circling against the spite of December's breath, ice blown through the wonky spaces of your toes — all ten lined up like a row of tatty soldiers, determined to stick out over the edge of life.

# What Death Said

Here the wind is too subtle, too unseen. Even the dew on the grass is safe, the ant's straight line over the slate and the slack wire line from tree to wall – even this is static, stock-still in the air. She waits for change, a sneeze or a sigh, some shift in the view. She does not trust or know nature like this – inanimacy, she finds, breeds a tension like death. For this, she is always unprepared, always taken back — to the night on a lost road, waiting out the surprise that comes when death pricks open her eyes and says: *you have known me before I have known you.*

# Ghost in the Stone

When she died, the silver chain was moved from one neck to another; the mother's skin now bare as well as cold, while the daughter's acquired a new heat and a strange pulse. The amber stone that pulled the chain into a V, warm again, jumped every so often against the uneven tremors of her chest. As the years passed, guilt grew less heavy around her neck, until one day she removed the chain, placed it in a box with other things, without thinking that her mother had just re-died, or even, that she had just killed her. All she had done, she reasoned, was to put her away, in a box that was safe, and unlikely to open on its own whenever she dreamt, spoke or thought about it.

# My Father's Garden

He bends to their heads in the ground; their faces under his shadow are midnight blue. 'Look at that dear, just look at that. In the grass. Tiny. What are they dear? No-one ever looks dear, ever does.' His shadow has caused a wind. Each petal twitches as if in smoulder. His body leans slightly closer towards the earth and he catches himself, just before the light vanishes altogether. The tremors of flowers are perceptible. The laughter of earth, sly.

# Family Portrait

My mother's death taught me language; I reward her in words. To the scratched music of her epilepsy I set the drills of upturned roads to sentences and crack ink across the pages. What splits into the white is not writing, not speech, but pieces of voice, littering the home, like smashed china.

\*

My father's sickness taught me calm. In the smoke from his pipe, and the wavering turn of his hand through the air as he conducted to the radio, I remember how the mouth sounds when closed over an object. A muffled bite of teeth on wood, followed by heaves, sighs and rushes of breath.

\*

My father's pipe offered a kind of twin to the wooden spoon we could never prise into my mother's mouth. And the soar of his smoke and hand told me that the noises I cannot spell were a part of something quiet; a calm to an unstitched song that fell apart in front of me and broke again inside.

# The Mending Wall

Walking in the door of one house, he appeared through the door of another. She sat on a bench in the garden, and timed her gaze accordingly: in no less than six circuits, she saw a twitch in the corner of his mouth, a smile, then heard a breath, a letter, a word and finally a sentence. Out of the door, down the steps, along the path, past the bench, on the sixth circle, he told her that 'b' was for brick. He took her back, to the wooden coloured blocks of her childhood. More than the structure, what she remembered of home in this hospital garden was the silence, the concentration, the toppled wood, the reconfigured colours, the frustration and the inability to speak until the building was over. When she looked up, the man raised a hand to her, half-mast, opened his mouth about a sound and disappeared through the second door. Once inside, swallowed by walls, she had exactly one minute to watch the wind, and a bee, enter the flowers – each force bending back their heads – exiting then beginning this delicate strike on the mouth of another. When the man had disappeared for the last time, he'd laughed over a light trip made in his slippers: *thoughtiwasgonethen*. She wanted to make sure he wouldn't go out altogether, like the light in her speechless mouth. She would keep him in her memory; a secure place made of stairs, windows, boards, ceilings, details and not just doors, one saying exit, the other, entrance. He had a chance of living on then, in her head – a third house where circles did not breed – where sentences made of words that went in one door and out the other, were stopped, attacked, arrested, broken and put back together again: taught lessons they'd never forget.

# Christ: Crouch End

*I'm just off to the end of the lawn, to have a fag with Jesus, dear.*

In the summer of an overgrown garden my tall, white-crowned father shuffled through brambles and flora in his slippers with the sole intention of sitting amidst the undergrowth with Jesus. Neck turtled forward, tea held at an angle, wetting his sleeves in splashes, pipe tobacco and Swan matches stuffed into the left pocket of his cords, he'd lowered himself into the wilderness, pressed flowers into the mud, and disappeared inside an idle brew of smoke and dandelion clocks. I didn't know my father when he'd conversed and smoked with the Lord. But I've known him since, and in the look of his hands conducting the dove grey coils and turns from his burning pipe, in the soft grain of his voice as he offers me tea, and the far shores that move in his eyes when he speaks, I can see him with his legs stretched out across the daisies. I can see his hand moving an untidy cigarette between his lap and his mouth, passing the breeze-blown hours, and I can feel and hear his head, warming and nodding under the sun, as Jesus listened, as much as he was listened to.

# The Prose Poem

That night, she got down on her hands and knees and placed a wolf in the middle of the floor. They watched as she encircled her prey, kept her eyes fixed on the victim, but viewed it from different angles as she moved around its still body. The room they were in began to change. She took away the walls and put oaks in their place. Switched lamps for a twilit wood. Lost the chairs, books, rugs, photos, table by the bay window, and the bay window itself. Stripped the living room of all this, and replaced the objects with smell. Sweet, dank musk with a quick sting of freshly drawn sap, after the rain had fallen through the leaves, meandered along the branches, down the bark, its rhythm slowed over the scars and ruptures, before it melded with the earth at the roots. Finally, she did away with herself – lost the feeling of being watched on the floor, thinning her trousers, skin bleeding at the joints, eyes dried out from unblinking.

# The Swallow Myth

Just before she entered the woods, she stopped and spent some time standing on the roadside worrying into the core of her apple, uneasy at the sight of leaves. Behind her, a crow skittered onto the branch of a tree – its polished eye, deadpan, seasonless, her own, bursting with life as she tried to fathom the tricks of a single leaf. When she walked through the gate, across the path between the trees, the pip of the apple moved down inside her throat. She felt the eyes of Elms, Willows and Oaks begin to watch her, as though they could see inside, knew how she would grow and what she would look like under the weight of birds and fruit. She heard the chatter and slur of green tongues telling her of limbs blistering into knots, the scars from beaks and claws, the bruises from falls, the rotting of colours, the blitz of weather, the onslaught of seasons, and the unsettling blindness of underground, treading the dark like water.

# Falling Out of the Wood

She spells it out carefully, burns it inside her head and tries to forget it. She agrees with herself that it was a dirty word, that it is important not to share it with anyone, not even herself anymore. In the mirror, she watches her face. Under her eyes the black of the word's ashes. She waits for them to fall down onto her tongue, at which point she'll empty out her head like a grate. Moving away from the glass and out of the door, she'll throw them in the direction of the wood. Once in the wind, they'll stick to the trees, grow irretrievable from the pine. Back inside she'll drown her mouth with water, swill out its soul and be able to start again. 'I'm clean', she'll say when she returns. 'A dirty word fell into me, and when I killed it I fell out of the wood, pure as pine.' 'Bullshit,' they'll say, 'absolute nonsense.' That's exactly how it all starts she'll fling back, turning to look behind her at the tap, tap, tap of wooden hands.

# Weather Quartet

Winter is a low-lit ending of a leaf.

Spring turns outwards, a pale-skinned face from a hood.

Summer is water hissing down a baked wall.

Autumn blushes from all its falling hair.

Each year,

they speak over one another.

# Station Butterflies

Kicked up from the tracks by wind from a passing train, butterflies flicker the air. In multiple shavings of suede, they burst above the station, race towards and away from each other, in the manner of moths grown wise to a candle. Leaves tremble at their passing; sometimes they swap characters, but mainly settle on mimicry. In between the trees, the sky is textured in shades of fawn, bark, and autumn. Underneath their swallow dives, weightless and hard to predict, her heart thunders into her feet. Another train moves towards them, slows in sight of the platform. A butterfly glints before the driver's window. She watches the sun explode on the glass, the man's face blanch, and catches the insect's wings as light scales a fish, hooked, upturned and thrashing between the sky and a river.

# Indoor Skies

He dipped a finger into the champagne glass and rubbed the drink into his mother's lips. Taking a freesia from the vase beside her head his wife placed the open petals under her nose, the flower covering her mouth, the colour moving in small shivers as she tried to talk. The youngest in the room, the grandchild, pushed a balloon towards her; the father gently brought it back. Birthday cards were opened and balanced upon her, winged, and tilting along the length of her body; in turns they were picked up and read aloud, hovered and resettled over the blanket. Near her head, a farmhouse, the courtyard detailed in feathers, uneven walls turning red from the roses. Below her shoulder, a car the colour of elm leaves, gliding country lanes between the hedgerows. On her stomach, a figure in white, the face shadowed in parasol. By her knees, a yellow cornfield, under the wind in song, and at her feet, orange poppies on a bank, laughing at something the river had said.

# Bridgesong

Those who stand, time their bow before the bridge with the confidence peculiar to habit. The others, cupping their wine, dip or arch their necks in response, as the punt floats through, slips into the arch of the old stone bridge. In the cool of its shadow, a shout, a glint of wine, the strike of glass. The tunnel begins to shake. Questions fight over lyrics; answers are thrown back for effect. They speak not to each other, but each to himself; listening to the way its age, damp from lack of light, the occasional cast of water, can change the human voice mid-song or conversation. Halfway through the dark, they stop quiet in its mouth and hear the dank hum of stone. Once out of silhouette, under the lowering evening sky, each figure comes to life, their features less clear this side of the stone, as the sun folds onto its reflection, leaves dusk in tiny drops over their glasses, and lights the inside of the boat as lamps bring life to a village. Black swans in the boat's wake and wine in the blood of the driver, the patterns of the water begin to change, the evening river growing a language of its own, surface at first but deepened with circles as the punt begins to spin. One by one the passengers pick out a ripple, a phrase from the worried tide, to wear upon their face and read each other anew.

# The Seasoned Listener

The audience are in winter; it is visible in their backs, in the hills they make that lower into the wind and wait for snow. They are stopped from the cold and the hunger bred by silence. They are tightly mooded, curled up in a half listen, the eyes turned inwards and the face down, the floor of the room cast back at them, dimming the skin with shadows. The author stands before them, opens his book, removes his hand from the blanketing of the pages, leans his head towards the print, peers over the view and opens his mouth. His story leaves him, with the apologetic gait of a new boy at school. The small crowd remain unmoved; the breath reserved, a small bare mist that comes and goes. The author moves towards the centre of the page. Men seen from the road play chess outside their doors; the game is balanced on a tilting table that follows the slant of the street; a light shout ensues from the slow slide of a chess piece. Over the page crickets set off their songs like laughter in the dark. Waves bruise the shore. The sky turns and reflects black over the sea. The air freezes. He leaves it there. Rises to show he has finished, and looks out from his book. Stretched before him is the ocean. The audience are gone. The room is pitch black and steel wintered. Something like an echo sounds itself out near his toes. He watches himself listening. Listens to himself watching.

# Hunger

She moves in over the land, picks a pebble from her last tide-line and swallows it whole. The earth stirs in grains. Wood baked light from a fire is siphoned from a shallow pit. High on the sandbank, an abandoned boat begins to expand – in a constant state of drying out, the blue paint splinters in the wind. The dye unfurls over the body, lifts off the wood in little hands. They beg towards the ocean. Stones are varnished with the slide of each wave; nothing dries before the next onslaught. The colours have a sound, of breath held in anticipation. Gulls puncture the air. Trees on the cliff begin to wrench up their roots – the branches tighten over the nests and the birds begin to shriek as the leaves fasten their wings. Sap glues over the bones and the birds begin to slow their fight. Below the land is disappearing; the beach pulled towards the sea like a rug heavy with objects. The effect is of a child's magic board, written on, pulled, then gone; written on, pulled, then gone.

# The Herd

Crossing between fields, they curl mist, and break the morning over their coats. Drops suspended between hairs glint then die in the low winter sun. The ground softens from their tread; under the weight the mud sings, and fur clots from the catch of notes. When they stop, the sound thickens in the air; between them softly blown speech moves with a graceful chaos. In stillness, words hammock among them, billowing from one face to another. The cobwebs of attics grow in the space of things; the incidental sew of chair, garment, and book. The mist floats like an after-phrase between the leathery muzzles of cows. Thoughts are adrift. The punctuation of a spider, a fly, is random and rare during the winters of meadows and lofts. Conversations like these, suspended in shrouds, are not about a subject, a heart, a focus. They are about themselves, and perhaps the borders at the edges that support them.

# The Handwritten

The throat closes at the smell: damp neglect in an old wooden room, hoarding unkempt letters, and the mildew of dropped thoughts. By the scuttle of mice and spiders a newfangled script lives inside the attic. In scratches, bites and shrouds, nature edits its library of ghosted hands; puts pay to skin, recollection and thought in a single hover over a line. The ink of a noun, a comma, a question, fades below the need of an animal; in manners like these, conversations change, and slip backwards into the paper. Elsewhere, by the windowless parts of the room, corners of suitcases and open drawers become warm and murky nests, the endless chatter of shreds oblivious to the lengthening shadows. At night, and when the moon is hidden behind clouds, their work is swallowed whole. In the mouths of the black unlit cases and drawers, there is the possibility that the original language is still there, bright and polished, the scent of blue ink still fresh from the nib. Then the door opens, the throat closes at the smell, and what is not seen, is heard, outside at first, then in.

# Little Sisyphus

The earth parts above its head and light pours through the hole like rain. Until now, the dark had been its roof. Then broken by a crown that could thread the eye of a needle, this smooth patch of mud is undone; unlevelled from below. In one burst, this lowly penny-sized plot of land is given character; from a single shove, a hill is formed; the effect barely more than a pin's journey through a wall, the plaster behind the paint opened into, the silt falling, moving and settling either side of the wound. Outside, the weight of sun and rock barely felt upon its back, the ant starts to build with the earth. In the journeys between one boulder of soil and the next, paths are being formed. The ant returns again and again to the same hill through crevices, drying lakes and a particularly windblown stretch. Soon the land starts to behave like a place; a setting without a name, where the ant goes about its business, deafening the world below as it works between the light and the dark, carrying the rocks to the top of the hill, grappling its mouth around the earth's crust, speaking all day in stone.

Dropping the sounds like bombs
and starting again.

# The Cry in the Wall

A cat with a white face was seen in the window of a dead man's address. Inside of absence, its voice began to peter out; a waterless crack of a cry, disappearing behind the door of a moth-eaten bedroom. The animal had been reported by a neighbour, who on being kept awake at night, stepped outside, and followed the sound up the wall towards the roof. Her neck fully craned, she found its face open with distress, lit softly by a streetlamp, gulping the amber glow through its eyes. Somewhere between the ill man's demise and the emptying of his house, life had gone and crept back in. For a while, officers worked along leads and threads, gathering them among the doors of his road by asking questions related to belonging and missing. Eventually the rooms worked back towards silence; the last voice starting to ghost in the neighbour's mouth. No one claimed, or entered at any point. Today, some do not hear it, while some wait patiently for the cry in the wall to fade. But others, it is said, shout over it, lose it, drop to their knees, and pray, beg, whisper for it to stop.

# Blood Cycle

In the shadow of a cat, the frog bends his face to my palm as to water, and prints a piece of red, the colour of a human cut, on my skin. One eye weeps, the other freezes blue, its shade drifting between the interior of a shell and the dying iris of an old woman. Around its slow beating heart, grass rises high and forms a briar like forest. The cat prowls its margins, and waits for movement again. I am in the middle of nature; a garden umpire refusing the hunter with one hand, urging the hunted to safety with the other. The frog moves once, and stops. In its wake, grass shivers, falls, bleeds.

# The Pale Glass Wall

The knife cuts the air and the room begins to seep. Objects gasp from the change. Breath, sky, space are gutted; she tries to stuff herself into the void, but someone holds her wrists and keeps her from disappearing. Cries outside the glass trouble the water around the fish. They try to let go of themselves, their trails complicating their movement, looping and shaking behind them like a closely watched signature. Outside the glass house, lights interchange until they cancel each other out. Her skin blinks on and off without rhythm. The darkness soon rubs her out; what isn't there pulses in the black. The blade continues to punctuate the atmosphere, unsure of its own ending.

# Alice Aphasia

Words kept vanishing or tripping on her tongue, as though she was going blind in the mouth. Inside her head, she knew they were there, sitting up in chairs, lounging on sofas, talking and eating at tables, satisfying whatever it was that they wanted. But when she parted her jaw, they scattered in all directions – wrecked beyond repair and recognition. The few that remained un-damaged, were either lost, or slipping in apology towards death. A blind Alice, she thought, whose mouth stumbled about things, too small, too large, or too strange, and whose sighs and yawns of despair bore the clout of hurricanes and blizzards. Just when silence seemed the only answer, she removed her tongue and put a pen in its place. Over time, she forgot to watch them. But they were all still there, her unseen slaves – banished from chairs, tables, lounging on sofas, swinging from lights, splitting from laughter – learning to satisfy whatever it was that she wanted.

# The Lesson

She has learnt to deflect ignorance, hold her own upon her heels, fix her eyes on the other and say: yes, I know, I know about that too. When the wind hurtles the leaves, upsets her hair and spills the strands over her face, she keeps her arms folded across her chest, waits for the weather to stop talking first. Shiftless. Resolute. A lighthouse indifferent to the thrash and climb of the sea at its walls. There is nothing to correct in her. When she was young she learnt that language was scaffold, that reason was upheld by a bolt around each word. Now she is older, she has learnt not to question structure – the consequences of flinching when birds attack, dark, mistaken, and unspellable.

# The Estranged

She stopped using her breath when she spoke. Words skittered from her mouth like pebbles. She considered the stone's last fall, how it would sink through the cold and gather darkness in the loom of its sleep; sit blind, mute and deaf until the fortune of a kick, a shift under the river-bed. She shivered. She would slow down. Take her language from a wooden boat, moving the soft edge of a lake; the grass, the wood, and water always touching. Others would step into her conversations with a sure foot, certain that everything around her anchored words was as it was, as it was supposed to be: in a boat, on a lake lit by the moon; a bright clear unruffled eye, under the steady tongue of the wind.

# Blackwater

Winter has arrived in the valley; a magician loosening the fibres of his cloak, the silence of his flight over the mountains, quickening the pace of wind and fall towards night until the layers grow about the cottage, as a rose blooms around its bud. Collecting wood, they talk about the valley, looking over their shoulders at Blackwater in its hours before the storm: the tilted land that bleats and moves with sheep, the fields that grow foggy then clear in patches – the breath around the heads of cows, the rivers and waterfalls that hurtle through gullies of stone and mud, giggling and bumping over figures and faces in the mountains, the low and insistent purr of tractors until at night, the velvet flurry of the owl's call. Winter has come like a magician, the Black Valley disappearing under his spell: the clear appointed eye of the moon, watchful as a shepherd, as a thousand guests of cold arrive, their footsteps settling the frost to a glittering skin of ice, binding roads to rocks, to trees, to lakes, to grasses. Windless and moonstruck both flower and house alike are forced to close, gather fire from the inside and wait the magician out.

# Speaking Without Tongues

Their conversation rustles in the manner of Edwardian skirts; the talk of the passengers around them clicks like the tap of heels. The sound of sign is of clouds snagging on trees, of a line cast over a river, the distant race of water heading across the stones, the catch of a glug as the stream falls between rocks. Shadows animate the train windows; they puppet the textures of silence, flight-ways of hands catch and knit words mid-air. Rings pick out the light like eyes. Outside, the mammoth breath of cows, the push of crows against the sky, the windblown climb of bough and leaf, the itch and sweep of rain and grass, etch out their talk till dark.

By night, their conversation twins in the glass.

# The Speaking Cloth

As she hid her mouth behind her hand, she recalled the woman with the scarf. Someone close to her, who shared her house and once her bed, had told her she was ugly; that her borrowed teeth unsettled conversations, that her mouth was without scaffolding, her face inarticulate, her skin the paper of creased-up thoughts. So, one day, as the sun rose and bled between the curtains in a clean gash of light, she took a floral cotton scarf and wound it around her neck and over her mouth. At the sound of his leaving, she appeared and spoke through the scarf, the front of the material puffing in and out according to the thoughts she'd had that day. As her throat fills with the wind and the flowers, she hears the sun, ticking carefully over her head.

# The Clock

The head of the man in front of me clatters with rage. Above him a china plate clock on the wall, the hands of which haven't yet moved from summer to winter. 'Get the cake,' he says. The woman doesn't answer, but tilts her face towards the ceiling to finish her glass. A small white round object tight with icing and coloured by letters appears. It is lit with four candles, and hovers above the palms of the waitress, her mouth half open as everyone starts to sing. When the song is over the boy leaps onto his seat and grimaces over the orange flames. It is his birthday and he is going to take time blowing out his age. He is not talking, but cackling; flinging his neck back and widening his eyes until their glow dims in the vanishing light. At the last puff, he picks up the knife and slices the cake under a small cloud of smoke. Everyone gets a letter. The man in front of me gets his own initial. With his left hand, he forks it, brings it to his mouth, and swallows it whole. His head stops shaking as he focuses on the wine; the way it chases the lump in his throat. In a minute, a thought will leave his mouth by accident.

# Peter's Pica

Some bring stone rather than potato to the mouth. Others weigh the stomach down as far as the hips with metal. For the pican, the world needs to be white, clear of things, safe; mattresses indestructible and flooring laminate, the skin of bears impenetrable. And when the child is broken, plasters must be kept in their box while the blood is left to dry in the air. This is Peter's pica. Inconsistent, Peter's mouth is always being watched; is suspect in stillness or in motion. Sand, pebbles, stones, cigarette ends, pen tops, the ends of plastic razors, string, sellotape. This list has gone beyond his tongue. As an adult, I wonder what he remembers: the taste of these objects; the action of ripping open his bear with his tiny limbs, his teeth staining from wounds, or the sensation of his young throat disappearing in a cloud of fibre.

# Unannounced Visitors

The sob spoke first – like the first sound of a baby, whacked on the back if born too silent – followed by water from her left eye. Yes, she thinks she was relieved; like giving birth through the mouth, she laughed. But then something worked its way back inside her: a magician, who plucks a small boy from the audience, stages him in the centre, draws objects with his hands from behind the boy's ear, and then opens his mouth to find a ball, the size of an egg. When this is removed and placed on a table, another appears. She continues to watch as lump after lump travels up the child, opens his mouth, and stops him from speaking.

# Kierkegaard's Chairs

When Kierkegaard was eight, his father made his son eavesdrop on the conversations of his dinner guests, then sit in each of their chairs after they had left. Nicknamed 'the fork', at home, because that was the object he named when asked what he'd like to be, the seated boy would be tested. The father wanted to hear each of the guest's arguments and thoughts through the mouth of his son, as though the boy was not just one man, but as many as ten. Almost word for word, 'the fork' recounted what these men had said, men who were among the finest thinkers in the city. The tale is chilling somehow. Not least because his father at the same age, raised his fists to the desolate sky of Jutland Heath, and cursed God for his suffering and fate. Not least because of the son sitting in each of those chairs, their backs straight and high, rising behind him like headstones, while the words of others poured from his mouth, his father at the head of the table, testing his son like God. Not least because when asked why he wanted to be a fork, Kierkegaard answered: "Well, then I could spear anything I wanted on the dinner table." And if he was chased? "Well then," he'd responded, "then I'd spear you."

# The Silent Trade

Objects are going missing in the house. The light, the long and thin, the cylindrical, the manageable, the stuff that sits easily in the palm, that's held between the fingers without strain, is being homed again. In the shade of a table, a chair, a rug, a gap in the wall, the used and the humble are reconfiguring. Clusters of mute and unlikely sets, tirelessly lost and found; dismantled and assembled again. In hiding, they listen to the dreams of the furniture; eavesdrop on the schemes of the wood. Upstairs the rugs whisper in plots. In the dining room, they hear of the old oak table, its double-edge; a land of exile and safety. Their world is determined; reliant on a forgetful God.

# Object Poem

We do not write about the object – we write about the shadow it casts or the reflection it throws back at us. We talk about the setting, the human dramas that crowd outside it. We try to know them all. The language. The disasters. We write about the wind that moves, throws, or breaks it, but ignore that so low to the ground, something like a stone can remain complete and still during the unhinged run of a hurricane, and that stillness of a tiny thing without so much of a flinch when nothing else stands a chance, is worth a thought at least. The words can follow later, in a mere handful, and that is something. Something at least, on which to build, or not, as the case may be.

# 'I, Poppy'

They've dug up the red from the mud, and replaced the heads with white. Flipped onto the bankside of the grass, their scarlet ears fold and bruise black at the edges. While they wait, they turn over as if in sleep, their pillarbox skin rusting and shivering in the grass, one ear juddering to the inconstancy of the wind. Gathered up by the gardener their features are torn, the chase of the ground, the journey towards the flower-pit seen through holes in the petals; red-framed eyes recording the hectic charge of his boot. On the heap, one more piece of damaged colour attempts something like breath. On forgetting, it stops with the rest, de-named against the wanton twists of landscape.

# Gutter-cup

The street is kinked and faceless; an untended canvas beneath the weather's pass. Random stains of clouds migrate like cows overhead. Sooted throws from trees and lamps stretch and die before they meet. The wind solidifies in shadow, falls into cracks and gasps, reappears from the tyres of a car, and slides unfettered from the weight. A turn in the breeze shakes things above the stones. A plastic cup is lifted skyward and kicked into submission. After the rain stops, the cup, split and doubled over, drags itself into the kerb, and rests in a cushion of mud. The approaching sun slips into the city, separates the shadowed from the lit, halts over an object, yawns fire, and watches it melt.

# Fossilized

Skin explodes across the mouth and seals it shut. Another follows, taut pale and pink, stretched white like a spider's abdomen. Sugared air splits from the shell and dies among the tatters. She peels the mess from her skin, stuffs it back inside. The teeth and tongue set to work again, defiantly forming bubbles. The voice bombs pink at the mouth, swells and snaps the end of her sentence. The tongue grows tired; matter hardens in the circularity of her movement, and loses its taste. The tension in her jaw tutors her language anew and the words grow arthritic, breaking early outside of her. Finally the thing grows cold, indifferent to her breath. She is left with a petrified mould, casting back the curt indents of her bite, the chaotic overlaps of language; a vestige of something trying to become told.

# Visible Speech

Once lit, these packed cuts of land, ease themselves away in smoke; return themselves to the earth in powder. Somewhere between the black side of conker, and the bourbon shade of soil, these tightly stitched fibres of mud are unsewn from the ground, and thrown among the twigs and logs of an untried hearth. At the quick scuff of a match, they become the fire's thrive; its thundering swallow, the aching bass line of the cottage's warmth. Outside, the tongue of the chimney conducts them back into the world again: escapees, cast-outs, ex-objects, re-named and unheld, they disappear mid-sentence, the sky their paper now.